BUDGET *Tracker*

BUDGET FOR MONTH OF

	TOTAL INCOME	**TOTAL BUDGET**	**TOTAL EXPENSES**
	$	$	$

100%	**BUDGET FOR**	**TOTAL USED**		**BUDGET**
		0%	100%	$
		0%	100%	$
		0%	100%	$
		0%	100%	$
		0%	100%	$
		0%	100%	$
		0%	100%	$
		0%	100%	$

TOTAL BUDGET USED

INCOME TRACKER

DATE	SOURCE	DESCRIPTION/ DETAILS	AMOUNT

Dedication:

This book is dedicated to all the Money Planners in the world.

You are my inspiration in producing books and I'm excite to help in the planning of all parts of your money life!

How to Use this book

The purpose of this book is to keep all your budgeting and financial plans and ideas organized in one easy to find spot. Here are some simple guidelines to follow so you can make the most of using this book:

1. Use the fill in the blank prompt pages in this planner to help navigate your savings and money goals. This will make it easy for you to keep everything organized!

2. The first "Budget Tracker" section is for you to write the "Budgeting Plan" so goals can be easily seen.

Most ideas are inspired by something we have seen. Use the "Savings Goal" section to color in the amounts of coins you are saving each month.

3. The "Expense Tracker" section is for you to detail out a description of your incoming and outgoing money.

Don't worry, there will be more space for you to go in-depth with space for notes.

4. Some information that you love to remember, are the "Monthly Budget Progress" is great for that. You will see the actual money spent, get closer to your goals you will love to record and make notes about!

5. Flip the page over and this is where your "Monthly Money Goals Tracker" begins.

Write down the action steps you need to complete your "Savings Chart" item saving for, cost and time frame.

6. The "52 week Money Savings Challenge" section is so you can visually track your goals and be inspired later after you finished!

7. Use The "Annual Overview" to find the perfect income, expenses, start balance and ending balance for the year.

8. And finally pages with your "Debt Repayment Plan" for you to journal about your new money life, brainstorm and watch your plans unfold...

Have fun!

MY SAVINGS GOAL

I WILL SAVE

EACH ○ REPRESENTS

Expense
TRACKER

MONTH OF:

DATE	DESCRIPTION	INCOME	OUTGOING

Total Income   Total Spent   Balance

MONTHLY BUDGET TRACKER

		MONTH

DATE	INCOME DESCRIPTION	AMOUNT EARNED

Fixed Expenses

DATE	DESCRIPTION	AMOUNT

Variable Expenses

DATE	DESCRIPTION	AMOUNT

	PLANNED	ACTUAL	DIFFERENCE + / -
EARNED			
SPENT			
SAVED			
DEBT			

MONTHLY BUDGET PROGRESS

MONTH

	GOAL	ACTUAL	DIFFERENCE + / -
EARNED			
SPENT			
SAVED			
DEBT			

CATEGORY:	AMOUNT SPENT
BUDGET:	TOTAL:

CATEGORY:	AMOUNT SPENT
BUDGET:	TOTAL:

CATEGORY:	AMOUNT SPENT
BUDGET:	TOTAL:

CATEGORY:	AMOUNT SPENT
BUDGET:	TOTAL:

MONTHLY BUDGET PLANNER

		MONTH

UTILITIES	BUDGET	SPENT
Electric		
Gas		
Water		
Internet		
Phone		
Total		

PERSONAL	BUDGET	SPENT
Entertainment		
Clothing		
Cosmetic		
Subscriptions		
Other		
Total		

HOME	BUDGET	SPENT
Rent / Mortgage		
Taxes		
Insurance		
Repairs		
Decor		
Total		

TRASPORTATION	BUDGET	SPENT
Car Payment		
Car Insurance		
Gas		
Maintance		
Public Transport		
Total		

FOOD / DRINKS	BUDGET	SPENT
Shopping / Groceries		
Eating out		
Drinks		
Total		

MEDICAL	BUDGET	SPENT
Doctor Bills		
Medication		
Other		
Total		

GIVING	BUDGET	SPENT
Birthday Gifts		
Charities		
Total		

DEBTS	BUDGET	SPENT
Credit Cards		
Other		
Total		

INCOME	AMOUNT	DATE

ACCOUNTS	START	FINISH

MONTHLY BUDGET PLANNER

		MONTH

UTILITIES	BUDGET	SPENT

PERSONAL	BUDGET	SPENT

HOME	BUDGET	SPENT

TRASPORTATION	BUDGET	SPENT

FOOD / DRINKS	BUDGET	SPENT

MEDICAL	BUDGET	SPENT

GIVING	BUDGET	SPENT

DEBTS	BUDGET	SPENT

INCOME	AMOUNT	DATE

ACCOUNTS	START	FINISH

MONTHLY MONEY GOALS TRACKER

MONTHLY MONEY GOALS	PROGRESS TRACKER			
1:	25%	50%	75%	100%
2:	25%	50%	75%	100%
3:	25%	50%	75%	100%
4:	25%	50%	75%	100%

WEEK	GOAL 1	GOAL 2	GOAL 3	GOAL 3
1				
2				
3				
4				

NOTES

NOTES	YES / NO
I set reasonable goals	
I met my budget goals	

MONTHLY SAVINGS PLAN

	MONTH

OPENING BALANCE	SAVINGS GOAL	SAVED

DATE	WITHDRAWAL / DEPOSIT

NOTES	REWARD

SAVINGS CHART

ITEM I AM SAVING FOR	COST	TIME FRAME

MONEY TRACKER		DATE	SAVED	BALANCE
100%				

75%				

50%				

25%				

NOTES

52 WEEK MONEY SAVING CHALLENGE

☑	WEEK	AMOUNT	BALANCE	☑	WEEK	AMOUNT	BALANCE
	1	$1	$1		27	$27	$378
	2	$2	$3		28	$28	$406
	3	$3	$6		29	$29	$435
	4	$4	$10		30	$30	$465
	5	$5	$15		31	$31	$496
	6	$6	$21		32	$32	$528
	7	$7	$28		33	$33	$561
	8	$8	$36		34	$34	$595
	9	$9	$45		35	$35	$630
	10	$10	$55		36	$36	$666
	11	$11	$66		37	$37	$703
	12	$12	$78		38	$38	$741
	13	$13	$91		39	$39	$780
	14	$14	$105		40	$40	$820
	15	$15	$120		41	$41	$861
	16	$16	$136		42	$42	$903
	17	$17	$153		43	$43	$946
	18	$18	$171		44	$44	$990
	19	$19	$190		45	$45	$1035
	20	$20	$210		46	$46	$1081
	21	$21	$231		47	$47	$1128
	22	$22	$253		48	$48	$1176
	23	$23	$276		49	$49	$1225
	24	$24	$300		50	$50	$1275
	25	$25	$325		51	$51	$1326
	26	$26	$351		52	$52	$1378

ANNUAL OVERVIEW

	INCOME	EXPENSES	SAVINGS	START BALANCE	END BALANCE
January					
February					
March					
April					
May					
June					
July					
August					
September					
October					
November					
December					
Total					

	MONTH	NOTES
Best month for income		
Lowest amount on expenses		
Highest amount of savings		
Worst month for income		
Highest amount on expenses		
Lowest amount on savings		

NOTES

2020 YEARLY PAYMENT OVERVIEW

ITEM	J	F	M	A	M	J	J	A	S	O	N	D

DEBT REPAYMENT PLAN

ACCOUNT	DUE DATE	MINIMUM DUE

CREDIT LIMIT	INTEREST RATE	CREDITOR

STARTING AMOUNT	TARGET PAYOFF DAY	ADDITIONAL INFORMATION

DATE	PAYMENT	BALANCE	NOTES

Bill Tracker

MONTH OF:

UTILITIES	BUDGET	SPENT
ELECTRIC	$	$
GAS	$	$
TRASH	$	$
INTERNET	$	$
PHONE	$	$
TOTAL	$	$

PERSONAL	BUDGET	SPENT
ENTERTAINMENT	$	$
CLOTHING	$	$
COSMETICS	$	$
LIFE INSURANCE	$	$
OTHER	$	$
TOTAL	$	$

HOME	BUDGET	SPENT
RENT/MORTGAGE	$	$
TAXES	$	$
INSURANCE	$	$
REPAIRS	$	$
TOTAL	$	$

TRANSPORTATION	BUDGET	SPENT
CAR PAYMENT	$	$
CAR INSURANCE	$	$
GAS	$	$
MAINTENANCE	$	$
TOTAL	$	$

FOOD	BUDGET	SPENT
GROCERIES	$	$
EATING OUT	$	$
TOTAL	$	$

MEDICAL	BUDGET	SPENT
DOCTOR BILLS	$	$
MEDICATION	$	$
TOTAL	$	$

GIVING	BUDGET	SPENT
TITHES	$	$
CHARITY	$	$
TOTAL	$	$

DEBTS	BUDGET	SPENT
CREDIT CARD	$	$
OTHER	$	$
TOTAL	$	$

INCOME

DATE	FROM WHERE?	AMT

CHECKING ACCOUNT

STARTING	GOAL	ENDING

SAVINGS ACCOUNT

STARTING	GOAL	ENDING

NOTES:

the monthly bill tracker

due	description	J F M A M J J A S O N D

Expense Tracker

MONTH OF:

date	description	category	amount	balance
				the total

Upcoming Expenses

JANUARY

- $ _____
- $ _____
- $ _____
- $ _____
- $ _____
- $ _____
- $ _____

FEBRUARY

- $ _____
- $ _____
- $ _____
- $ _____
- $ _____
- $ _____
- $ _____

MARCH

- $ _____
- $ _____
- $ _____
- $ _____
- $ _____
- $ _____
- $ _____

APRIL

- $ _____
- $ _____
- $ _____
- $ _____
- $ _____
- $ _____
- $ _____

MAY

- $ _____
- $ _____
- $ _____
- $ _____
- $ _____
- $ _____
- $ _____

JUNE

- $ _____
- $ _____
- $ _____
- $ _____
- $ _____
- $ _____
- $ _____

JULY

- $ _____
- $ _____
- $ _____
- $ _____
- $ _____
- $ _____
- $ _____

AUGUST

- $ _____
- $ _____
- $ _____
- $ _____
- $ _____
- $ _____
- $ _____

SEPTEMBER

- $ _____
- $ _____
- $ _____
- $ _____
- $ _____
- $ _____
- $ _____

OCTOBER

- $ _____
- $ _____
- $ _____
- $ _____
- $ _____
- $ _____
- $ _____

NOVEMBER

- $ _____
- $ _____
- $ _____
- $ _____
- $ _____
- $ _____
- $ _____

DECEMBER

- $ _____
- $ _____
- $ _____
- $ _____
- $ _____
- $ _____
- $ _____

Tax Checklist

INCOME

GENERAL

ADJUSTMENTS / CREDIT

PAID TAXES

RETIREMENT

MEDICAL

CHARITABLE

MISC / EXTRAS

BUDGET *Tracker*

BUDGET FOR MONTH OF	TOTAL INCOME	TOTAL BUDGET	TOTAL EXPENSES
	$	$	$

100%

BUDGET FOR	TOTAL USED		BUDGET
	0%	100%	$
	0%	100%	$
	0%	100%	$
	0%	100%	$
	0%	100%	$
	0%	100%	$
	0%	100%	$
	0%	100%	$

TOTAL BUDGET USED

INCOME TRACKER

DATE	SOURCE	DESCRIPTION: DETAILS	AMOUNT

MY SAVINGS GOAL

I WILL SAVE

EACH ◯ REPRESENTS

Expense
TRACKER

MONTH OF:

DATE	DESCRIPTION	INCOME	OUTGOING

Total Income   *Total Spent*   *Balance*

MONTHLY BUDGET TRACKER

	MONTH

DATE	INCOME DESCRIPTION	AMOUNT EARNED

Fixed Expenses

DATE	DESCRIPTION	AMOUNT

Variable Expenses

DATE	DESCRIPTION	AMOUNT

	PLANNED	ACTUAL	DIFFERENCE + / -
EARNED			
SPENT			
SAVED			
DEBT			

MONTHLY BUDGET PROGRESS

	GOAL	ACTUAL	DIFFERENCE + / -
EARNED			
SPENT			
SAVED			
DEBT			

CATEGORY:	AMOUNT SPENT	CATEGORY:	AMOUNT SPENT
BUDGET:	TOTAL:	BUDGET:	TOTAL:

CATEGORY:	AMOUNT SPENT	CATEGORY:	AMOUNT SPENT
BUDGET:	TOTAL:	BUDGET:	TOTAL:

MONTHLY BUDGET PLANNER

		MONTH

UTILITIES	BUDGET	SPENT
Electric		
Gas		
Water		
Internet		
Phone		
Total		

PERSONAL	BUDGET	SPENT
Entertainment		
Clothing		
Cosmetic		
Subscriptions		
Other		
Total		

HOME	BUDGET	SPENT
Rent / Mortgage		
Taxes		
Insurance		
Repairs		
Decor		
Total		

TRASPORTATION	BUDGET	SPENT
Car Payment		
Car Insurance		
Gas		
Maintance		
Public Transport		
Total		

FOOD / DRINKS	BUDGET	SPENT
Shopping / Groceries		
Eating out		
Drinks		
Total		

MEDICAL	BUDGET	SPENT
Doctor Bills		
Medication		
Other		
Total		

GIVING	BUDGET	SPENT
Birthday Gifts		
Charities		
Total		

DEBTS	BUDGET	SPENT
Credit Cards		
Other		
Total		

INCOME	AMOUNT	DATE

ACCOUNTS	START	FINISH

MONTHLY BUDGET PLANNER

| | | MONTH |

UTILITIES	BUDGET	SPENT

PERSONAL	BUDGET	SPENT

HOME	BUDGET	SPENT

TRASPORTATION	BUDGET	SPENT

FOOD / DRINKS	BUDGET	SPENT

MEDICAL	BUDGET	SPENT

GIVING	BUDGET	SPENT

DEBTS	BUDGET	SPENT

INCOME	AMOUNT	DATE

ACCOUNTS	START	FINISH

MONTHLY MONEY GOALS TRACKER

MONTHLY MONEY GOALS	PROGRESS TRACKER			
1:	25%	50%	75%	100%
2:	25%	50%	75%	100%
3:	25%	50%	75%	100%
4:	25%	50%	75%	100%

WEEK	GOAL 1	GOAL 2	GOAL 3	GOAL 3
1				
2				
3				
4				

NOTES

NOTES	YES / NO
I set reasonable goals	
I met my budget goals	

MONTHLY SAVINGS PLAN

	MONTH

OPENING BALANCE	SAVINGS GOAL	SAVED

DATE	WITHDRAWAL / DEPOSIT

NOTES	REWARD

SAVINGS CHART

ITEM I AM SAVING FOR	COST	TIME FRAME

MONEY TRACKER		DATE	SAVED	BALANCE
100% ----				
75% ----				
50% ----				
25% ----				

NOTES

52 WEEK MONEY SAVING CHALLENGE

☑	WEEK	AMOUNT	BALANCE	☑	WEEK	AMOUNT	BALANCE
	1	$1	$1		27	$27	$378
	2	$2	$3		28	$28	$406
	3	$3	$6		29	$29	$435
	4	$4	$10		30	$30	$465
	5	$5	$15		31	$31	$496
	6	$6	$21		32	$32	$528
	7	$7	$28		33	$33	$561
	8	$8	$36		34	$34	$595
	9	$9	$45		35	$35	$630
	10	$10	$55		36	$36	$666
	11	$11	$66		37	$37	$703
	12	$12	$78		38	$38	$741
	13	$13	$91		39	$39	$780
	14	$14	$105		40	$40	$820
	15	$15	$120		41	$41	$861
	16	$16	$136		42	$42	$903
	17	$17	$153		43	$43	$946
	18	$18	$171		44	$44	$990
	19	$19	$190		45	$45	$1035
	20	$20	$210		46	$46	$1081
	21	$21	$231		47	$47	$1128
	22	$22	$253		48	$48	$1176
	23	$23	$276		49	$49	$1225
	24	$24	$300		50	$50	$1275
	25	$25	$325		51	$51	$1326
	26	$26	$351		52	$52	$1378

ANNUAL OVERVIEW

	INCOME	EXPENSES	SAVINGS	START BALANCE	END BALANCE
January					
February					
March					
April					
May					
June					
July					
August					
September					
October					
November					
December					
Total					

	MONTH	NOTES
Best month for income		
Lowest amount on expenses		
Highest amount of savings		
Worst month for income		
Highest amount on expenses		
Lowest amount on savings		

NOTES

2020 YEARLY PAYMENT OVERVIEW

ITEM	J	F	M	A	M	J	J	A	S	O	N	D

DEBT REPAYMENT PLAN

ACCOUNT	DUE DATE	MINIMUM DUE

CREDIT LIMIT	INTEREST RATE	CREDITOR

STARTING AMOUNT	TARGET PAYOFF DAY	ADDITIONAL INFORMATION

DATE	PAYMENT	BALANCE	NOTES

MONTH OF:

UTILITIES	BUDGET	SPENT
ELECTRIC	$	$
GAS	$	$
TRASH	$	$
INTERNET	$	$
PHONE	$	$
TOTAL	$	$

PERSONAL	BUDGET	SPENT
ENTERTAINMENT	$	$
CLOTHING	$	$
COSMETICS	$	$
LIFE INSURANCE	$	$
OTHER	$	$
TOTAL	$	$

HOME	BUDGET	SPENT
RENT/MORTGAGE	$	$
TAXES	$	$
INSURANCE	$	$
REPAIRS	$	$
TOTAL	$	$

TRANSPORTATION	BUDGET	SPENT
CAR PAYMENT	$	$
CAR INSURANCE	$	$
GAS	$	$
MAINTENANCE	$	$
TOTAL	$	$

FOOD	BUDGET	SPENT
GROCERIES	$	$
EATING OUT	$	$
TOTAL	$	$

MEDICAL	BUDGET	SPENT
DOCTOR BILLS	$	$
MEDICATION	$	$
TOTAL	$	$

GIVING	BUDGET	SPENT
TITHES	$	$
CHARITY	$	$
TOTAL	$	$

DEBTS	BUDGET	SPENT
CREDIT CARD	$	$
OTHER	$	$
TOTAL	$	$

INCOME		
DATE	FROM WHERE?	AMT

CHECKING ACCOUNT

STARTING	GOAL	ENDING

SAVINGS ACCOUNT

STARTING	GOAL	ENDING

NOTES:

the monthly bill tracker

due	description	J	F	M	A	M	J	J	A	S	O	N	D

Expense Tracker

MONTH OF:

date	description	category	amount	balance
			the total	

Upcoming Expenses

JANUARY
$
$
$
$
$
$
$

FEBRUARY
$
$
$
$
$
$
$

MARCH
$
$
$
$
$
$
$

APRIL
$
$
$
$
$
$
$

MAY
$
$
$
$
$
$
$

JUNE
$
$
$
$
$
$
$

JULY
$
$
$
$
$
$
$

AUGUST
$
$
$
$
$
$
$

SEPTEMBER
$
$
$
$
$
$
$

OCTOBER
$
$
$
$
$
$
$

NOVEMBER
$
$
$
$
$
$
$

DECEMBER
$
$
$
$
$
$
$

Tax Checklist

INCOME

GENERAL

ADJUSTMENTS / CREDIT

PAID TAXES

RETIREMENT

MEDICAL

CHARITABLE

MISC / EXTRAS

BUDGET *Tracker*

BUDGET FOR MONTH OF		TOTAL INCOME	TOTAL BUDGET	TOTAL EXPENSES
		$	$	$

100%

BUDGET FOR	TOTAL USED		BUDGET
	0%	100%	$
	0%	100%	$
	0%	100%	$
	0%	100%	$
	0%	100%	$
	0%	100%	$
	0%	100%	$
	0%	100%	$

TOTAL BUDGET USED

INCOME TRACKER

DATE	SOURCE	DESCRIPTION DETAILS	AMOUNT

MY SAVINGS GOAL

I WILL SAVE

EACH  REPRESENTS

Expense
TRACKER

MONTH OF:

DATE	DESCRIPTION	INCOME	OUTGOING

Total Income   *Total Spent*   *Balance*

MONTHLY BUDGET TRACKER

		MONTH

DATE	INCOME DESCRIPTION	AMOUNT EARNED

Fixed Expenses

DATE	DESCRIPTION	AMOUNT

Variable Expenses

DATE	DESCRIPTION	AMOUNT

	PLANNED	ACTUAL	DIFFERENCE + / -
EARNED			
SPENT			
SAVED			
DEBT			

MONTHLY BUDGET PROGRESS

	GOAL	ACTUAL	DIFFERENCE + / -
EARNED			
SPENT			
SAVED			
DEBT			

CATEGORY:	AMOUNT SPENT	CATEGORY:	AMOUNT SPENT
BUDGET:	TOTAL:	BUDGET:	TOTAL:

CATEGORY:	AMOUNT SPENT	CATEGORY:	AMOUNT SPENT
BUDGET:	TOTAL:	BUDGET:	TOTAL:

MONTHLY BUDGET PLANNER

		MONTH

UTILITIES	BUDGET	SPENT
Electric		
Gas		
Water		
Internet		
Phone		
Total		

PERSONAL	BUDGET	SPENT
Entertainment		
Clothing		
Cosmetic		
Subscriptions		
Other		
Total		

HOME	BUDGET	SPENT
Rent / Mortgage		
Taxes		
Insurance		
Repairs		
Decor		
Total		

TRASPORTATION	BUDGET	SPENT
Car Payment		
Car Insurance		
Gas		
Maintance		
Public Transport		
Total		

FOOD / DRINKS	BUDGET	SPENT
Shopping / Groceries		
Eating out		
Drinks		
Total		

MEDICAL	BUDGET	SPENT
Doctor Bills		
Medication		
Other		
Total		

GIVING	BUDGET	SPENT
Birthday Gifts		
Charities		
Total		

DEBTS	BUDGET	SPENT
Credit Cards		
Other		
Total		

INCOME	AMOUNT	DATE

ACCOUNTS	START	FINISH

MONTHLY BUDGET PLANNER

		MONTH

UTILITIES	BUDGET	SPENT

PERSONAL	BUDGET	SPENT

HOME	BUDGET	SPENT

TRASPORTATION	BUDGET	SPENT

FOOD / DRINKS	BUDGET	SPENT

MEDICAL	BUDGET	SPENT

GIVING	BUDGET	SPENT

DEBTS	BUDGET	SPENT

INCOME	AMOUNT	DATE

ACCOUNTS	START	FINISH

MONTHLY MONEY GOALS TRACKER

MONTHLY MONEY GOALS	PROGRESS TRACKER			
1:	25%	50%	75%	100%
2:	25%	50%	75%	100%
3:	25%	50%	75%	100%
4:	25%	50%	75%	100%

WEEK	GOAL 1	GOAL 2	GOAL 3	GOAL 3
1				
2				
3				
4				

NOTES	NOTES	YES / NO
	I set reasonable goals	
	I met my budget goals	

MONTHLY SAVINGS PLAN

MONTH

OPENING BALANCE	SAVINGS GOAL	SAVED

DATE	WITHDRAWAL / DEPOSIT

NOTES	REWARD

SAVINGS CHART

ITEM I AM SAVING FOR	COST	TIME FRAME

MONEY TRACKER		DATE	SAVED	BALANCE
100%				

75%				

50%				

25%				

NOTES

52 WEEK MONEY SAVING CHALLENGE

☑	WEEK	AMOUNT	BALANCE
	1	$1	$1
	2	$2	$3
	3	$3	$6
	4	$4	$10
	5	$5	$15
	6	$6	$21
	7	$7	$28
	8	$8	$36
	9	$9	$45
	10	$10	$55
	11	$11	$66
	12	$12	$78
	13	$13	$91
	14	$14	$105
	15	$15	$120
	16	$16	$136
	17	$17	$153
	18	$18	$171
	19	$19	$190
	20	$20	$210
	21	$21	$231
	22	$22	$253
	23	$23	$276
	24	$24	$300
	25	$25	$325
	26	$26	$351

☑	WEEK	AMOUNT	BALANCE
	27	$27	$378
	28	$28	$406
	29	$29	$435
	30	$30	$465
	31	$31	$496
	32	$32	$528
	33	$33	$561
	34	$34	$595
	35	$35	$630
	36	$36	$666
	37	$37	$703
	38	$38	$741
	39	$39	$780
	40	$40	$820
	41	$41	$861
	42	$42	$903
	43	$43	$946
	44	$44	$990
	45	$45	$1035
	46	$46	$1081
	47	$47	$1128
	48	$48	$1176
	49	$49	$1225
	50	$50	$1275
	51	$51	$1326
	52	$52	$1378

ANNUAL OVERVIEW

	INCOME	EXPENSES	SAVINGS	START BALANCE	END BALANCE
January					
February					
March					
April					
May					
June					
July					
August					
September					
October					
November					
December					
Total					

	MONTH	NOTES
Best month for income		
Lowest amount on expenses		
Highest amount of savings		
Worst month for income		
Highest amount on expenses		
Lowest amount on savings		

NOTES

2020 YEARLY PAYMENT OVERVIEW

ITEM	J	F	M	A	M	J	J	A	S	O	N	D

DEBT REPAYMENT PLAN

ACCOUNT	DUE DATE	MINIMUM DUE

CREDIT LIMIT	INTEREST RATE	CREDITOR

STARTING AMOUNT	TARGET PAYOFF DAY	ADDITIONAL INFORMATION

DATE	PAYMENT	BALANCE	NOTES

Bill Tracker

MONTH OF:

UTILITIES	BUDGET	SPENT
ELECTRIC	$	$
GAS	$	$
TRASH	$	$
INTERNET	$	$
PHONE	$	$
TOTAL	$	$

PERSONAL	BUDGET	SPENT
ENTERTAINMENT	$	$
CLOTHING	$	$
COSMETICS	$	$
LIFE INSURANCE	$	$
OTHER	$	$
TOTAL	$	$

HOME	BUDGET	SPENT
RENT/MORTGAGE	$	$
TAXES	$	$
INSURANCE	$	$
REPAIRS	$	$
TOTAL	$	$

TRANSPORTATION	BUDGET	SPENT
CAR PAYMENT	$	$
CAR INSURANCE	$	$
GAS	$	$
MAINTENANCE	$	$
TOTAL	$	$

FOOD	BUDGET	SPENT
GROCERIES	$	$
EATING OUT	$	$
TOTAL	$	$

MEDICAL	BUDGET	SPENT
DOCTOR BILLS	$	$
MEDICATION	$	$
TOTAL	$	$

GIVING	BUDGET	SPENT
TITHES	$	$
CHARITY	$	$
TOTAL	$	$

DEBTS	BUDGET	SPENT
CREDIT CARD	$	$
OTHER	$	$
TOTAL	$	$

INCOME

DATE	FROM WHERE?	AMT

CHECKING ACCOUNT

STARTING	GOAL	ENDING

SAVINGS ACCOUNT

STARTING	GOAL	ENDING

NOTES:

the monthly bill tracker

due	description	J	F	M	A	M	J	J	A	S	O	N	D

Expense Tracker

MONTH OF:

date	description	category	amount	balance
			the total	

Upcoming Expenses

JANUARY

- $
- $
- $
- $
- $
- $
- $

FEBRUARY

- $
- $
- $
- $
- $
- $
- $

MARCH

- $
- $
- $
- $
- $
- $
- $

APRIL

- $
- $
- $
- $
- $
- $
- $

MAY

- $
- $
- $
- $
- $
- $
- $

JUNE

- $
- $
- $
- $
- $
- $
- $

JULY

- $
- $
- $
- $
- $
- $
- $

AUGUST

- $
- $
- $
- $
- $
- $
- $

SEPTEMBER

- $
- $
- $
- $
- $
- $
- $

OCTOBER

- $
- $
- $
- $
- $
- $
- $

NOVEMBER

- $
- $
- $
- $
- $
- $
- $

DECEMBER

- $
- $
- $
- $
- $
- $
- $

Tax Checklist

INCOME

GENERAL

ADJUSTMENTS / CREDIT

PAID TAXES

RETIREMENT

MEDICAL

CHARITABLE

MISC / EXTRAS

BUDGET *Tracker*

BUDGET FOR MONTH OF	TOTAL INCOME	TOTAL BUDGET	TOTAL EXPENSES
	$	$	$

100%

BUDGET FOR		TOTAL USED		BUDGET
	0%		100%	$
	0%		100%	$
	0%		100%	$
	0%		100%	$
	0%		100%	$
	0%		100%	$
	0%		100%	$
	0%		100%	$

TOTAL BUDGET USED

INCOME TRACKER

DATE	SOURCE	DESCRIPTION DETAILS	AMOUNT

MY SAVINGS GOAL

I WILL SAVE

EACH  REPRESENTS

Expense
TRACKER

MONTH OF:

DATE	DESCRIPTION	INCOME	OUTGOING

Total Income   *Total Spent*   *Balance*

MONTHLY BUDGET TRACKER

		MONTH

DATE	INCOME DESCRIPTION	AMOUNT EARNED

Fixed Expenses

DATE	DESCRIPTION	AMOUNT

Variable Expenses

DATE	DESCRIPTION	AMOUNT

	PLANNED	ACTUAL	DIFFERENCE + / -
EARNED			
SPENT			
SAVED			
DEBT			

MONTHLY BUDGET PROGRESS

	MONTH

	GOAL	ACTUAL	DIFFERENCE + / -
EARNED			
SPENT			
SAVED			
DEBT			

CATEGORY:	AMOUNT SPENT
BUDGET:	TOTAL:

CATEGORY:	AMOUNT SPENT
BUDGET:	TOTAL:

CATEGORY:	AMOUNT SPENT
BUDGET:	TOTAL:

CATEGORY:	AMOUNT SPENT
BUDGET:	TOTAL:

MONTHLY BUDGET PLANNER

		MONTH

UTILITIES	BUDGET	SPENT
Electric		
Gas		
Water		
Internet		
Phone		
Total		

PERSONAL	BUDGET	SPENT
Entertainment		
Clothing		
Cosmetic		
Subscriptions		
Other		
Total		

HOME	BUDGET	SPENT
Rent / Mortgage		
Taxes		
Insurance		
Repairs		
Decor		
Total		

TRASPORTATION	BUDGET	SPENT
Car Payment		
Car Insurance		
Gas		
Maintance		
Public Transport		
Total		

FOOD / DRINKS	BUDGET	SPENT
Shopping / Groceries		
Eating out		
Drinks		
Total		

MEDICAL	BUDGET	SPENT
Doctor Bills		
Medication		
Other		
Total		

GIVING	BUDGET	SPENT
Birthday Gifts		
Charities		
Total		

DEBTS	BUDGET	SPENT
Credit Cards		
Other		
Total		

INCOME	AMOUNT	DATE

ACCOUNTS	START	FINISH

MONTHLY BUDGET PLANNER

		MONTH

UTILITIES	BUDGET	SPENT

PERSONAL	BUDGET	SPENT

HOME	BUDGET	SPENT

TRASPORTATION	BUDGET	SPENT

FOOD / DRINKS	BUDGET	SPENT

MEDICAL	BUDGET	SPENT

GIVING	BUDGET	SPENT

DEBTS	BUDGET	SPENT

INCOME	AMOUNT	DATE

ACCOUNTS	START	FINISH

MONTHLY MONEY GOALS TRACKER

MONTHLY MONEY GOALS	PROGRESS TRACKER			
1:	25%	50%	75%	100%
2:	25%	50%	75%	100%
3:	25%	50%	75%	100%
4:	25%	50%	75%	100%

WEEK	GOAL 1	GOAL 2	GOAL 3	GOAL 3
1				
2				
3				
4				

NOTES

NOTES	YES / NO
I set reasonable goals	
I met my budget goals	

MONTHLY SAVINGS PLAN

	MONTH

OPENING BALANCE	SAVINGS GOAL	SAVED

DATE	WITHDRAWAL / DEPOSIT

NOTES	REWARD

SAVINGS CHART

ITEM I AM SAVING FOR	COST	TIME FRAME

MONEY TRACKER		DATE	SAVED	BALANCE
100%				

75%				

50%				

25%				

NOTES

52 WEEK MONEY SAVING CHALLENGE

☑	WEEK	AMOUNT	BALANCE	☑	WEEK	AMOUNT	BALANCE
	1	$1	$1		27	$27	$378
	2	$2	$3		28	$28	$406
	3	$3	$6		29	$29	$435
	4	$4	$10		30	$30	$465
	5	$5	$15		31	$31	$496
	6	$6	$21		32	$32	$528
	7	$7	$28		33	$33	$561
	8	$8	$36		34	$34	$595
	9	$9	$45		35	$35	$630
	10	$10	$55		36	$36	$666
	11	$11	$66		37	$37	$703
	12	$12	$78		38	$38	$741
	13	$13	$91		39	$39	$780
	14	$14	$105		40	$40	$820
	15	$15	$120		41	$41	$861
	16	$16	$136		42	$42	$903
	17	$17	$153		43	$43	$946
	18	$18	$171		44	$44	$990
	19	$19	$190		45	$45	$1035
	20	$20	$210		46	$46	$1081
	21	$21	$231		47	$47	$1128
	22	$22	$253		48	$48	$1176
	23	$23	$276		49	$49	$1225
	24	$24	$300		50	$50	$1275
	25	$25	$325		51	$51	$1326
	26	$26	$351		52	$52	$1378

ANNUAL OVERVIEW

	INCOME	EXPENSES	SAVINGS	START BALANCE	END BALANCE
January					
February					
March					
April					
May					
June					
July					
August					
September					
October					
November					
December					
Total					

	MONTH	NOTES
Best month for income		
Lowest amount on expenses		
Highest amount of savings		
Worst month for income		
Highest amount on expenses		
Lowest amount on savings		

NOTES

2020 YEARLY PAYMENT OVERVIEW

ITEM	J	F	M	A	M	J	J	A	S	O	N	D

DEBT REPAYMENT PLAN

ACCOUNT	DUE DATE	MINIMUM DUE

CREDIT LIMIT	INTEREST RATE	CREDITOR

STARTING AMOUNT	TARGET PAYOFF DAY	ADDITIONAL INFORMATION

DATE	PAYMENT	BALANCE	NOTES

Bill Tracker

MONTH OF: [   ]

UTILITIES	BUDGET	SPENT
ELECTRIC	$	$
GAS	$	$
TRASH	$	$
INTERNET	$	$
PHONE	$	$
TOTAL	$	$

PERSONAL	BUDGET	SPENT
ENTERTAINMENT	$	$
CLOTHING	$	$
COSMETICS	$	$
LIFE INSURANCE	$	$
OTHER	$	$
TOTAL	$	$

HOME	BUDGET	SPENT
RENT/MORTGAGE	$	$
TAXES	$	$
INSURANCE	$	$
REPAIRS	$	$
TOTAL	$	$

TRANSPORTATION	BUDGET	SPENT
CAR PAYMENT	$	$
CAR INSURANCE	$	$
GAS	$	$
MAINTENANCE	$	$
TOTAL	$	$

FOOD	BUDGET	SPENT
GROCERIES	$	$
EATING OUT	$	$
TOTAL	$	$

MEDICAL	BUDGET	SPENT
DOCTOR BILLS	$	$
MEDICATION	$	$
TOTAL	$	$

GIVING	BUDGET	SPENT
TITHES	$	$
CHARITY	$	$
TOTAL	$	$

DEBTS	BUDGET	SPENT
CREDIT CARD	$	$
OTHER	$	$
TOTAL	$	$

INCOME

DATE	FROM WHERE?	AMT

CHECKING ACCOUNT

STARTING	GOAL	ENDING

SAVINGS ACCOUNT

STARTING	GOAL	ENDING

NOTES:

the monthly bill tracker

due	description	J	F	M	A	M	J	J	A	S	O	N	D

Expense Tracker

date	description	category	amount	balance
			the total	

Upcoming Expenses

JANUARY

_____	$ _____
_____	$ _____
_____	$ _____
_____	$ _____
_____	$ _____
_____	$ _____
_____	$ _____

FEBRUARY

_____	$ _____
_____	$ _____
_____	$ _____
_____	$ _____
_____	$ _____
_____	$ _____
_____	$ _____

MARCH

_____	$ _____
_____	$ _____
_____	$ _____
_____	$ _____
_____	$ _____
_____	$ _____
_____	$ _____

APRIL

_____	$ _____
_____	$ _____
_____	$ _____
_____	$ _____
_____	$ _____
_____	$ _____
_____	$ _____

MAY

_____	$ _____
_____	$ _____
_____	$ _____
_____	$ _____
_____	$ _____
_____	$ _____
_____	$ _____

JUNE

_____	$ _____
_____	$ _____
_____	$ _____
_____	$ _____
_____	$ _____
_____	$ _____
_____	$ _____

JULY

_____	$ _____
_____	$ _____
_____	$ _____
_____	$ _____
_____	$ _____
_____	$ _____
_____	$ _____

AUGUST

_____	$ _____
_____	$ _____
_____	$ _____
_____	$ _____
_____	$ _____
_____	$ _____
_____	$ _____

SEPTEMBER

_____	$ _____
_____	$ _____
_____	$ _____
_____	$ _____
_____	$ _____
_____	$ _____
_____	$ _____

OCTOBER

_____	$ _____
_____	$ _____
_____	$ _____
_____	$ _____
_____	$ _____
_____	$ _____
_____	$ _____

NOVEMBER

_____	$ _____
_____	$ _____
_____	$ _____
_____	$ _____
_____	$ _____
_____	$ _____
_____	$ _____

DECEMBER

_____	$ _____
_____	$ _____
_____	$ _____
_____	$ _____
_____	$ _____
_____	$ _____
_____	$ _____

Tax Checklist

INCOME

GENERAL

ADJUSTMENTS / CREDIT

PAID TAXES

RETIREMENT

MEDICAL

CHARITABLE

MISC / EXTRAS

BUDGET *Tracker*

BUDGET FOR MONTH OF	TOTAL INCOME	TOTAL BUDGET	TOTAL EXPENSES
	$	$	$

100%

BUDGET FOR	TOTAL USED	BUDGET
	0%	100% $
	0%	100% $
	0%	100% $
	0%	100% $
	0%	100% $
	0%	100% $
	0%	100% $
	0%	100% $

TOTAL BUDGET USED

INCOME TRACKER

DATE	SOURCE	DESCRIPTION/ DETAILS	AMOUNT

MY SAVINGS GOAL

I WILL SAVE

EACH ◯ REPRESENTS

Expense
TRACKER

MONTH OF:

DATE	DESCRIPTION	INCOME	OUTGOING

Total Income   *Total Spent*   *Balance*

MONTHLY BUDGET TRACKER

	MONTH

DATE	INCOME DESCRIPTION	AMOUNT EARNED

Fixed Expenses

DATE	DESCRIPTION	AMOUNT

Variable Expenses

DATE	DESCRIPTION	AMOUNT

	PLANNED	ACTUAL	DIFFERENCE + / -
EARNED			
SPENT			
SAVED			
DEBT			

MONTHLY BUDGET PROGRESS

	GOAL	ACTUAL	DIFFERENCE + / -
EARNED			
SPENT			
SAVED			
DEBT			

CATEGORY:	AMOUNT SPENT
BUDGET:	TOTAL:

CATEGORY:	AMOUNT SPENT
BUDGET:	TOTAL:

CATEGORY:	AMOUNT SPENT
BUDGET:	TOTAL:

CATEGORY:	AMOUNT SPENT
BUDGET:	TOTAL:

MONTHLY BUDGET PLANNER

		MONTH

UTILITIES	BUDGET	SPENT
Electric		
Gas		
Water		
Internet		
Phone		
Total		

PERSONAL	BUDGET	SPENT
Entertainment		
Clothing		
Cosmetic		
Subscriptions		
Other		
Total		

HOME	BUDGET	SPENT
Rent / Mortgage		
Taxes		
Insurance		
Repairs		
Decor		
Total		

TRASPORTATION	BUDGET	SPENT
Car Payment		
Car Insurance		
Gas		
Maintance		
Public Transport		
Total		

FOOD / DRINKS	BUDGET	SPENT
Shopping / Groceries		
Eating out		
Drinks		
Total		

MEDICAL	BUDGET	SPENT
Doctor Bills		
Medication		
Other		
Total		

GIVING	BUDGET	SPENT
Birthday Gifts		
Charities		
Total		

DEBTS	BUDGET	SPENT
Credit Cards		
Other		
Total		

INCOME	AMOUNT	DATE

ACCOUNTS	START	FINISH

MONTHLY BUDGET PLANNER

		MONTH

UTILITIES	BUDGET	SPENT

PERSONAL	BUDGET	SPENT

HOME	BUDGET	SPENT

TRASPORTATION	BUDGET	SPENT

FOOD / DRINKS	BUDGET	SPENT

MEDICAL	BUDGET	SPENT

GIVING	BUDGET	SPENT

DEBTS	BUDGET	SPENT

INCOME	AMOUNT	DATE

ACCOUNTS	START	FINISH

MONTHLY MONEY GOALS TRACKER

MONTHLY MONEY GOALS	PROGRESS TRACKER			
1:	25%	50%	75%	100%
2:	25%	50%	75%	100%
3:	25%	50%	75%	100%
4:	25%	50%	75%	100%

WEEK	GOAL 1	GOAL 2	GOAL 3	GOAL 3
1				
2				
3				
4				

NOTES		NOTES	YES / NO
		I set reasonable goals	
		I met my budget goals	

MONTHLY SAVINGS PLAN

MONTH

OPENING BALANCE	SAVINGS GOAL	SAVED

DATE	WITHDRAWAL / DEPOSIT

NOTES	REWARD

SAVINGS CHART

ITEM I AM SAVING FOR	COST	TIME FRAME

MONEY TRACKER	DATE	SAVED	BALANCE
100%			

75%			

50%			

25%			

NOTES

52 WEEK MONEY SAVING CHALLENGE

☑	WEEK	AMOUNT	BALANCE	☑	WEEK	AMOUNT	BALANCE
	1	$1	$1		27	$27	$378
	2	$2	$3		28	$28	$406
	3	$3	$6		29	$29	$435
	4	$4	$10		30	$30	$465
	5	$5	$15		31	$31	$496
	6	$6	$21		32	$32	$528
	7	$7	$28		33	$33	$561
	8	$8	$36		34	$34	$595
	9	$9	$45		35	$35	$630
	10	$10	$55		36	$36	$666
	11	$11	$66		37	$37	$703
	12	$12	$78		38	$38	$741
	13	$13	$91		39	$39	$780
	14	$14	$105		40	$40	$820
	15	$15	$120		41	$41	$861
	16	$16	$136		42	$42	$903
	17	$17	$153		43	$43	$946
	18	$18	$171		44	$44	$990
	19	$19	$190		45	$45	$1035
	20	$20	$210		46	$46	$1081
	21	$21	$231		47	$47	$1128
	22	$22	$253		48	$48	$1176
	23	$23	$276		49	$49	$1225
	24	$24	$300		50	$50	$1275
	25	$25	$325		51	$51	$1326
	26	$26	$351		52	$52	$1378

ANNUAL OVERVIEW

	INCOME	EXPENSES	SAVINGS	START BALANCE	END BALANCE
January					
February					
March					
April					
May					
June					
July					
August					
September					
October					
November					
December					
Total					

	MONTH	NOTES
Best month for income		
Lowest amount on expenses		
Highest amount of savings		
Worst month for income		
Highest amount on expenses		
Lowest amount on savings		

NOTES

2020 YEARLY PAYMENT OVERVIEW

ITEM	J	F	M	A	M	J	J	A	S	O	N	D

DEBT REPAYMENT PLAN

ACCOUNT	DUE DATE	MINIMUM DUE

CREDIT LIMIT	INTEREST RATE	CREDITOR

STARTING AMOUNT	TARGET PAYOFF DAY	ADDITIONAL INFORMATION

DATE	PAYMENT	BALANCE	NOTES

Bill Tracker

MONTH OF:

UTILITIES	BUDGET	SPENT
ELECTRIC	$	$
GAS	$	$
TRASH	$	$
INTERNET	$	$
PHONE	$	$
TOTAL	$	$

PERSONAL	BUDGET	SPENT
ENTERTAINMENT	$	$
CLOTHING	$	$
COSMETICS	$	$
LIFE INSURANCE	$	$
OTHER	$	$
TOTAL	$	$

HOME	BUDGET	SPENT
RENT/MORTGAGE	$	$
TAXES	$	$
INSURANCE	$	$
REPAIRS	$	$
TOTAL	$	$

TRANSPORTATION	BUDGET	SPENT
CAR PAYMENT	$	$
CAR INSURANCE	$	$
GAS	$	$
MAINTENANCE	$	$
TOTAL	$	$

FOOD	BUDGET	SPENT
GROCERIES	$	$
EATING OUT	$	$
TOTAL	$	$

MEDICAL	BUDGET	SPENT
DOCTOR BILLS	$	$
MEDICATION	$	$
TOTAL	$	$

GIVING	BUDGET	SPENT
TITHES	$	$
CHARITY	$	$
TOTAL	$	$

DEBTS	BUDGET	SPENT
CREDIT CARD	$	$
OTHER	$	$
TOTAL	$	$

INCOME

DATE	FROM WHERE?	AMT

CHECKING ACCOUNT

STARTING	GOAL	ENDING

SAVINGS ACCOUNT

STARTING	GOAL	ENDING

NOTES:

the monthly bill tracker

due	description	J	F	M	A	M	J	J	A	S	O	N	D

Expense Tracker

MONTH OF:

date	description	category	amount	balance
			the total	

Upcoming Expenses

JANUARY

- $
- $
- $
- $
- $
- $
- $

FEBRUARY

- $
- $
- $
- $
- $
- $
- $

MARCH

- $
- $
- $
- $
- $
- $
- $

APRIL

- $
- $
- $
- $
- $
- $
- $

MAY

- $
- $
- $
- $
- $
- $
- $

JUNE

- $
- $
- $
- $
- $
- $
- $

JULY

- $
- $
- $
- $
- $
- $
- $

AUGUST

- $
- $
- $
- $
- $
- $
- $

SEPTEMBER

- $
- $
- $
- $
- $
- $
- $

OCTOBER

- $
- $
- $
- $
- $
- $
- $

NOVEMBER

- $
- $
- $
- $
- $
- $
- $

DECEMBER

- $
- $
- $
- $
- $
- $
- $

Tax Checklist

INCOME

- ○
- ○
- ○
- ○
- ○
- ○
- ○
- ○

GENERAL

- ○
- ○
- ○
- ○
- ○
- ○
- ○
- ○

ADJUSTMENTS / CREDIT

- ○
- ○
- ○
- ○
- ○
- ○
- ○
- ○

PAID TAXES

- ○
- ○
- ○
- ○
- ○
- ○
- ○
- ○

RETIREMENT

- ○
- ○
- ○
- ○
- ○
- ○
- ○
- ○

MEDICAL

- ○
- ○
- ○
- ○
- ○
- ○
- ○
- ○

CHARITABLE

- ○
- ○
- ○
- ○
- ○
- ○
- ○
- ○

MISC / EXTRAS

- ○
- ○
- ○
- ○
- ○
- ○
- ○
- ○

BUDGET *Tracker*

BUDGET FOR MONTH OF	TOTAL INCOME	TOTAL BUDGET	TOTAL EXPENSES
	$	$	$

100%

BUDGET FOR	TOTAL USED		BUDGET
	0%	100%	$
	0%	100%	$
	0%	100%	$
	0%	100%	$
	0%	100%	$
	0%	100%	$
	0%	100%	$
	0%	100%	$

TOTAL BUDGET USED

INCOME TRACKER

DATE	SOURCE	DESCRIPTION¦ DETAILS	AMOUNT

MY SAVINGS GOAL

I WILL SAVE

EACH ◯ REPRESENTS

Expense
TRACKER

MONTH OF:

DATE	DESCRIPTION	INCOME	OUTGOING

Total Income   *Total Spent*   *Balance*

MONTHLY BUDGET TRACKER

	MONTH

DATE	INCOME DESCRIPTION	AMOUNT EARNED

Fixed Expenses

DATE	DESCRIPTION	AMOUNT

Variable Expenses

DATE	DESCRIPTION	AMOUNT

	PLANNED	ACTUAL	DIFFERENCE + / -
EARNED			
SPENT			
SAVED			
DEBT			

MONTHLY BUDGET PROGRESS

	MONTH

	GOAL	ACTUAL	DIFFERENCE + / -
EARNED			
SPENT			
SAVED			
DEBT			

CATEGORY:	AMOUNT SPENT
BUDGET:	TOTAL:

CATEGORY:	AMOUNT SPENT
BUDGET:	TOTAL:

CATEGORY:	AMOUNT SPENT
BUDGET:	TOTAL:

CATEGORY:	AMOUNT SPENT
BUDGET:	TOTAL:

MONTHLY BUDGET PLANNER

		MONTH

UTILITIES	BUDGET	SPENT
Electric		
Gas		
Water		
Internet		
Phone		
Total		

PERSONAL	BUDGET	SPENT
Entertainment		
Clothing		
Cosmetic		
Subscriptions		
Other		
Total		

HOME	BUDGET	SPENT
Rent / Mortgage		
Taxes		
Insurance		
Repairs		
Decor		
Total		

TRASPORTATION	BUDGET	SPENT
Car Payment		
Car Insurance		
Gas		
Maintance		
Public Transport		
Total		

FOOD / DRINKS	BUDGET	SPENT
Shopping / Groceries		
Eating out		
Drinks		
Total		

MEDICAL	BUDGET	SPENT
Doctor Bills		
Medication		
Other		
Total		

GIVING	BUDGET	SPENT
Birthday Gifts		
Charities		
Total		

DEBTS	BUDGET	SPENT
Credit Cards		
Other		
Total		

INCOME	AMOUNT	DATE

ACCOUNTS	START	FINISH

MONTHLY BUDGET PLANNER

		MONTH

UTILITIES	BUDGET	SPENT

PERSONAL	BUDGET	SPENT

HOME	BUDGET	SPENT

TRASPORTATION	BUDGET	SPENT

FOOD / DRINKS	BUDGET	SPENT

MEDICAL	BUDGET	SPENT

GIVING	BUDGET	SPENT

DEBTS	BUDGET	SPENT

INCOME	AMOUNT	DATE

ACCOUNTS	START	FINISH

MONTHLY MONEY GOALS TRACKER

MONTHLY MONEY GOALS	PROGRESS TRACKER			
1:	25%	50%	75%	100%
2:	25%	50%	75%	100%
3:	25%	50%	75%	100%
4:	25%	50%	75%	100%

WEEK	GOAL 1	GOAL 2	GOAL 3	GOAL 3
1				
2				
3				
4				

NOTES		NOTES	YES / NO
		I set reasonable goals	
		I met my budget goals	

MONTHLY SAVINGS PLAN

	MONTH

OPENING BALANCE	SAVINGS GOAL	SAVED

DATE	WITHDRAWAL / DEPOSIT

NOTES	REWARD

SAVINGS CHART

ITEM I AM SAVING FOR	COST	TIME FRAME

MONEY TRACKER		DATE	SAVED	BALANCE
100%				

75%				

50%				

25%				

NOTES

52 WEEK MONEY SAVING CHALLENGE

☑	WEEK	AMOUNT	BALANCE	☑	WEEK	AMOUNT	BALANCE
	1	$ 1	$ 1		27	$ 27	$ 378
	2	$ 2	$ 3		28	$ 28	$ 406
	3	$ 3	$ 6		29	$ 29	$ 435
	4	$ 4	$ 10		30	$ 30	$ 465
	5	$ 5	$ 15		31	$ 31	$ 496
	6	$ 6	$ 21		32	$ 32	$ 528
	7	$ 7	$ 28		33	$ 33	$ 561
	8	$ 8	$ 36		34	$ 34	$ 595
	9	$ 9	$ 45		35	$ 35	$ 630
	10	$ 10	$ 55		36	$ 36	$ 666
	11	$ 11	$ 66		37	$ 37	$ 703
	12	$ 12	$ 78		38	$ 38	$ 741
	13	$ 13	$ 91		39	$ 39	$ 780
	14	$ 14	$ 105		40	$ 40	$ 820
	15	$ 15	$ 120		41	$ 41	$ 861
	16	$ 16	$ 136		42	$ 42	$ 903
	17	$ 17	$ 153		43	$ 43	$ 946
	18	$ 18	$ 171		44	$ 44	$ 990
	19	$ 19	$ 190		45	$ 45	$ 1035
	20	$ 20	$ 210		46	$ 46	$ 1081
	21	$ 21	$ 231		47	$ 47	$ 1128
	22	$ 22	$ 253		48	$ 48	$ 1176
	23	$ 23	$ 276		49	$ 49	$ 1225
	24	$ 24	$ 300		50	$ 50	$ 1275
	25	$ 25	$ 325		51	$ 51	$ 1326
	26	$ 26	$ 351		52	$ 52	$ 1378

ANNUAL OVERVIEW

	INCOME	EXPENSES	SAVINGS	START BALANCE	END BALANCE
January					
February					
March					
April					
May					
June					
July					
August					
September					
October					
November					
December					
Total					

	MONTH	NOTES
Best month for income		
Lowest amount on expenses		
Highest amount of savings		
Worst month for income		
Highest amount on expenses		
Lowest amount on savings		

NOTES

2020 YEARLY PAYMENT OVERVIEW

ITEM	J	F	M	A	M	J	J	A	S	O	N	D

DEBT REPAYMENT PLAN

ACCOUNT	DUE DATE	MINIMUM DUE

CREDIT LIMIT	INTEREST RATE	CREDITOR

STARTING AMOUNT	TARGET PAYOFF DAY	ADDITIONAL INFORMATION

DATE	PAYMENT	BALANCE	NOTES

Bill Tracker

MONTH OF: _____

UTILITIES	BUDGET	SPENT		PERSONAL	BUDGET	SPENT
ELECTRIC	$	$		ENTERTAINMENT	$	$
GAS	$	$		CLOTHING	$	$
TRASH	$	$		COSMETICS	$	$
INTERNET	$	$		LIFE INSURANCE	$	$
PHONE	$	$		OTHER	$	$
TOTAL	$	$		TOTAL	$	$

HOME	BUDGET	SPENT		TRANSPORTATION	BUDGET	SPENT
RENT/MORTGAGE	$	$		CAR PAYMENT	$	$
TAXES	$	$		CAR INSURANCE	$	$
INSURANCE	$	$		GAS	$	$
REPAIRS	$	$		MAINTENANCE	$	$
TOTAL	$	$		TOTAL	$	$

FOOD	BUDGET	SPENT		MEDICAL	BUDGET	SPENT
GROCERIES	$	$		DOCTOR BILLS	$	$
EATING OUT	$	$		MEDICATION	$	$
TOTAL	$	$		TOTAL	$	$

GIVING	BUDGET	SPENT		DEBTS	BUDGET	SPENT
TITHES	$	$		CREDIT CARD	$	$
CHARITY	$	$		OTHER	$	$
TOTAL	$	$		TOTAL	$	$

INCOME

DATE	FROM WHERE?	AMT

CHECKING ACCOUNT

STARTING	GOAL	ENDING

SAVINGS ACCOUNT

STARTING	GOAL	ENDING

NOTES:

the monthly bill tracker

due	description	J	F	M	A	M	J	J	A	S	O	N	D

Expense Tracker

MONTH OF:

date	description	category	amount	balance
			the total	

Upcoming Expenses

JANUARY

- _____ $ ____
- _____ $ ____
- _____ $ ____
- _____ $ ____
- _____ $ ____
- _____ $ ____
- _____ $ ____

FEBRUARY

- _____ $ ____
- _____ $ ____
- _____ $ ____
- _____ $ ____
- _____ $ ____
- _____ $ ____
- _____ $ ____

MARCH

- _____ $ ____
- _____ $ ____
- _____ $ ____
- _____ $ ____
- _____ $ ____
- _____ $ ____
- _____ $ ____

APRIL

- _____ $ ____
- _____ $ ____
- _____ $ ____
- _____ $ ____
- _____ $ ____
- _____ $ ____
- _____ $ ____

MAY

- _____ $ ____
- _____ $ ____
- _____ $ ____
- _____ $ ____
- _____ $ ____
- _____ $ ____
- _____ $ ____

JUNE

- _____ $ ____
- _____ $ ____
- _____ $ ____
- _____ $ ____
- _____ $ ____
- _____ $ ____
- _____ $ ____

JULY

- _____ $ ____
- _____ $ ____
- _____ $ ____
- _____ $ ____
- _____ $ ____
- _____ $ ____
- _____ $ ____

AUGUST

- _____ $ ____
- _____ $ ____
- _____ $ ____
- _____ $ ____
- _____ $ ____
- _____ $ ____
- _____ $ ____

SEPTEMBER

- _____ $ ____
- _____ $ ____
- _____ $ ____
- _____ $ ____
- _____ $ ____
- _____ $ ____
- _____ $ ____

OCTOBER

- _____ $ ____
- _____ $ ____
- _____ $ ____
- _____ $ ____
- _____ $ ____
- _____ $ ____
- _____ $ ____

NOVEMBER

- _____ $ ____
- _____ $ ____
- _____ $ ____
- _____ $ ____
- _____ $ ____
- _____ $ ____
- _____ $ ____

DECEMBER

- _____ $ ____
- _____ $ ____
- _____ $ ____
- _____ $ ____
- _____ $ ____
- _____ $ ____
- _____ $ ____

Tax Checklist

INCOME

GENERAL

ADJUSTMENTS / CREDIT

PAID TAXES

RETIREMENT

MEDICAL

CHARITABLE

MISC / EXTRAS

BUDGET *Tracker*

BUDGET FOR MONTH OF	TOTAL INCOME	TOTAL BUDGET	TOTAL EXPENSES
	$	$	$

100%

BUDGET FOR	TOTAL USED		BUDGET
	0%	100%	$
	0%	100%	$
	0%	100%	$
	0%	100%	$
	0%	100%	$
	0%	100%	$
	0%	100%	$
	0%	100%	$

TOTAL BUDGET USED

INCOME TRACKER

DATE	SOURCE	DESCRIPTION/ DETAILS	AMOUNT

MY SAVINGS GOAL

I WILL SAVE

EACH ◯ REPRESENTS

Expense
TRACKER

MONTH OF:

DATE	DESCRIPTION	INCOME	OUTGOING

Total Income   *Total Spent*   *Balance*

MONTHLY BUDGET TRACKER

		MONTH

DATE	INCOME DESCRIPTION	AMOUNT EARNED

Fixed Expenses

DATE	DESCRIPTION	AMOUNT

Variable Expenses

DATE	DESCRIPTION	AMOUNT

	PLANNED	ACTUAL	DIFFERENCE + / -
EARNED			
SPENT			
SAVED			
DEBT			

MONTHLY BUDGET PROGRESS

		MONTH

	GOAL	ACTUAL	DIFFERENCE + / -
EARNED			
SPENT			
SAVED			
DEBT			

CATEGORY:	AMOUNT SPENT
BUDGET:	TOTAL:

CATEGORY:	AMOUNT SPENT
BUDGET:	TOTAL:

CATEGORY:	AMOUNT SPENT
BUDGET:	TOTAL:

CATEGORY:	AMOUNT SPENT
BUDGET:	TOTAL:

MONTHLY BUDGET PLANNER

	MONTH

UTILITIES	BUDGET	SPENT
Electric		
Gas		
Water		
Internet		
Phone		
Total		

PERSONAL	BUDGET	SPENT
Entertainment		
Clothing		
Cosmetic		
Subscriptions		
Other		
Total		

HOME	BUDGET	SPENT
Rent / Mortgage		
Taxes		
Insurance		
Repairs		
Decor		
Total		

TRASPORTATION	BUDGET	SPENT
Car Payment		
Car Insurance		
Gas		
Maintance		
Public Transport		
Total		

FOOD / DRINKS	BUDGET	SPENT
Shopping / Groceries		
Eating out		
Drinks		
Total		

MEDICAL	BUDGET	SPENT
Doctor Bills		
Medication		
Other		
Total		

GIVING	BUDGET	SPENT
Birthday Gifts		
Charities		
Total		

DEBTS	BUDGET	SPENT
Credit Cards		
Other		
Total		

INCOME	AMOUNT	DATE

ACCOUNTS	START	FINISH

MONTHLY BUDGET PLANNER

MONTH

UTILITIES	BUDGET	SPENT

PERSONAL	BUDGET	SPENT

HOME	BUDGET	SPENT

TRASPORTATION	BUDGET	SPENT

FOOD / DRINKS	BUDGET	SPENT

MEDICAL	BUDGET	SPENT

GIVING	BUDGET	SPENT

DEBTS	BUDGET	SPENT

INCOME	AMOUNT	DATE

ACCOUNTS	START	FINISH

MONTHLY MONEY GOALS TRACKER

MONTHLY MONEY GOALS	PROGRESS TRACKER			
1:	25%	50%	75%	100%
2:	25%	50%	75%	100%
3:	25%	50%	75%	100%
4:	25%	50%	75%	100%

WEEK	GOAL 1	GOAL 2	GOAL 3	GOAL 3
1				
2				
3				
4				

NOTES

NOTES	YES / NO
I set reasonable goals	
I met my budget goals	

MONTHLY SAVINGS PLAN

	MONTH

OPENING BALANCE	SAVINGS GOAL	SAVED

DATE	WITHDRAWAL / DEPOSIT

NOTES	REWARD

SAVINGS CHART

ITEM I AM SAVING FOR	COST	TIME FRAME

MONEY TRACKER	DATE	SAVED	BALANCE

100%	

75%	

50%	

25%	

NOTES

52 WEEK MONEY SAVING CHALLENGE

☑	WEEK	AMOUNT	BALANCE	☑	WEEK	AMOUNT	BALANCE
	1	$1	$1		27	$27	$378
	2	$2	$3		28	$28	$406
	3	$3	$6		29	$29	$435
	4	$4	$10		30	$30	$465
	5	$5	$15		31	$31	$496
	6	$6	$21		32	$32	$528
	7	$7	$28		33	$33	$561
	8	$8	$36		34	$34	$595
	9	$9	$45		35	$35	$630
	10	$10	$55		36	$36	$666
	11	$11	$66		37	$37	$703
	12	$12	$78		38	$38	$741
	13	$13	$91		39	$39	$780
	14	$14	$105		40	$40	$820
	15	$15	$120		41	$41	$861
	16	$16	$136		42	$42	$903
	17	$17	$153		43	$43	$946
	18	$18	$171		44	$44	$990
	19	$19	$190		45	$45	$1035
	20	$20	$210		46	$46	$1081
	21	$21	$231		47	$47	$1128
	22	$22	$253		48	$48	$1176
	23	$23	$276		49	$49	$1225
	24	$24	$300		50	$50	$1275
	25	$25	$325		51	$51	$1326
	26	$26	$351		52	$52	$1378

ANNUAL OVERVIEW

	INCOME	EXPENSES	SAVINGS	START BALANCE	END BALANCE
January					
February					
March					
April					
May					
June					
July					
August					
September					
October					
November					
December					
Total					

	MONTH	NOTES
Best month for income		
Lowest amount on expenses		
Highest amount of savings		
Worst month for income		
Highest amount on expenses		
Lowest amount on savings		

NOTES

2020 YEARLY PAYMENT OVERVIEW

ITEM	J	F	M	A	M	J	J	A	S	O	N	D

DEBT REPAYMENT PLAN

ACCOUNT	DUE DATE	MINIMUM DUE

CREDIT LIMIT	INTEREST RATE	CREDITOR

STARTING AMOUNT	TARGET PAYOFF DAY	ADDITIONAL INFORMATION

DATE	PAYMENT	BALANCE	NOTES

Bill Tracker

MONTH OF:

UTILITIES	BUDGET	SPENT
ELECTRIC	$	$
GAS	$	$
TRASH	$	$
INTERNET	$	$
PHONE	$	$
TOTAL	$	$

PERSONAL	BUDGET	SPENT
ENTERTAINMENT	$	$
CLOTHING	$	$
COSMETICS	$	$
LIFE INSURANCE	$	$
OTHER	$	$
TOTAL	$	$

HOME	BUDGET	SPENT
RENT/MORTGAGE	$	$
TAXES	$	$
INSURANCE	$	$
REPAIRS	$	$
TOTAL	$	$

TRANSPORTATION	BUDGET	SPENT
CAR PAYMENT	$	$
CAR INSURANCE	$	$
GAS	$	$
MAINTENANCE	$	$
TOTAL	$	$

FOOD	BUDGET	SPENT
GROCERIES	$	$
EATING OUT	$	$
TOTAL	$	$

MEDICAL	BUDGET	SPENT
DOCTOR BILLS	$	$
MEDICATION	$	$
TOTAL	$	$

GIVING	BUDGET	SPENT
TITHES	$	$
CHARITY	$	$
TOTAL	$	$

DEBTS	BUDGET	SPENT
CREDIT CARD	$	$
OTHER	$	$
TOTAL	$	$

INCOME

DATE	FROM WHERE?	AMT

CHECKING ACCOUNT

STARTING	GOAL	ENDING

SAVINGS ACCOUNT

STARTING	GOAL	ENDING

NOTES:

the monthly bill tracker

due	description	J	F	M	A	M	J	J	A	S	O	N	D

Expense Tracker

MONTH OF:

date	description	category	amount	balance

the total

Upcoming Expenses

JANUARY
- _____ $ _____
- _____ $ _____
- _____ $ _____
- _____ $ _____
- _____ $ _____
- _____ $ _____
- _____ $ _____

FEBRUARY
- _____ $ _____
- _____ $ _____
- _____ $ _____
- _____ $ _____
- _____ $ _____
- _____ $ _____
- _____ $ _____

MARCH
- _____ $ _____
- _____ $ _____
- _____ $ _____
- _____ $ _____
- _____ $ _____
- _____ $ _____
- _____ $ _____

APRIL
- _____ $ _____
- _____ $ _____
- _____ $ _____
- _____ $ _____
- _____ $ _____
- _____ $ _____
- _____ $ _____

MAY
- _____ $ _____
- _____ $ _____
- _____ $ _____
- _____ $ _____
- _____ $ _____
- _____ $ _____
- _____ $ _____

JUNE
- _____ $ _____
- _____ $ _____
- _____ $ _____
- _____ $ _____
- _____ $ _____
- _____ $ _____
- _____ $ _____

JULY
- _____ $ _____
- _____ $ _____
- _____ $ _____
- _____ $ _____
- _____ $ _____
- _____ $ _____
- _____ $ _____

AUGUST
- _____ $ _____
- _____ $ _____
- _____ $ _____
- _____ $ _____
- _____ $ _____
- _____ $ _____
- _____ $ _____

SEPTEMBER
- _____ $ _____
- _____ $ _____
- _____ $ _____
- _____ $ _____
- _____ $ _____
- _____ $ _____
- _____ $ _____

OCTOBER
- _____ $ _____
- _____ $ _____
- _____ $ _____
- _____ $ _____
- _____ $ _____
- _____ $ _____
- _____ $ _____

NOVEMBER
- _____ $ _____
- _____ $ _____
- _____ $ _____
- _____ $ _____
- _____ $ _____
- _____ $ _____
- _____ $ _____

DECEMBER
- _____ $ _____
- _____ $ _____
- _____ $ _____
- _____ $ _____
- _____ $ _____
- _____ $ _____

Tax Checklist

INCOME

GENERAL

ADJUSTMENTS / CREDIT

PAID TAXES

RETIREMENT

MEDICAL

CHARITABLE

MISC / EXTRAS

BUDGET *Tracker*

BUDGET FOR MONTH OF	TOTAL INCOME	TOTAL BUDGET	TOTAL EXPENSES
	$	$	$

100%	BUDGET FOR		TOTAL USED		BUDGET
		0%		100%	$
		0%		100%	$
		0%		100%	$
		0%		100%	$
		0%		100%	$
		0%		100%	$
		0%		100%	$
		0%		100%	$

TOTAL BUDGET USED

INCOME TRACKER

DATE	SOURCE	DESCRIPTION/DETAILS	AMOUNT

MY SAVINGS GOAL

I WILL SAVE   EACH ◯ REPRESENTS

Expense
TRACKER

MONTH OF:

DATE	DESCRIPTION	INCOME	OUTGOING

Total Income   Total Spent   Balance

MONTHLY BUDGET TRACKER

	MONTH

DATE	INCOME DESCRIPTION	AMOUNT EARNED

Fixed Expenses

DATE	DESCRIPTION	AMOUNT

Variable Expenses

DATE	DESCRIPTION	AMOUNT

	PLANNED	ACTUAL	DIFFERENCE + / -
EARNED			
SPENT			
SAVED			
DEBT			

MONTHLY BUDGET PROGRESS

	MONTH

	GOAL	ACTUAL	DIFFERENCE + / -
EARNED			
SPENT			
SAVED			
DEBT			

CATEGORY:	AMOUNT SPENT
BUDGET:	TOTAL:

CATEGORY:	AMOUNT SPENT
BUDGET:	TOTAL:

CATEGORY:	AMOUNT SPENT
BUDGET:	TOTAL:

CATEGORY:	AMOUNT SPENT
BUDGET:	TOTAL:

MONTHLY BUDGET PLANNER

		MONTH

UTILITIES	BUDGET	SPENT
Electric		
Gas		
Water		
Internet		
Phone		
Total		

PERSONAL	BUDGET	SPENT
Entertainment		
Clothing		
Cosmetic		
Subscriptions		
Other		
Total		

HOME	BUDGET	SPENT
Rent / Mortgage		
Taxes		
Insurance		
Repairs		
Decor		
Total		

TRASPORTATION	BUDGET	SPENT
Car Payment		
Car Insurance		
Gas		
Maintance		
Public Transport		
Total		

FOOD / DRINKS	BUDGET	SPENT
Shopping / Groceries		
Eating out		
Drinks		
Total		

MEDICAL	BUDGET	SPENT
Doctor Bills		
Medication		
Other		
Total		

GIVING	BUDGET	SPENT
Birthday Gifts		
Charities		
Total		

DEBTS	BUDGET	SPENT
Credit Cards		
Other		
Total		

INCOME	AMOUNT	DATE

ACCOUNTS	START	FINISH

MONTHLY BUDGET PLANNER

		MONTH

UTILITIES	BUDGET	SPENT

PERSONAL	BUDGET	SPENT

HOME	BUDGET	SPENT

TRASPORTATION	BUDGET	SPENT

FOOD / DRINKS	BUDGET	SPENT

MEDICAL	BUDGET	SPENT

GIVING	BUDGET	SPENT

DEBTS	BUDGET	SPENT

INCOME	AMOUNT	DATE

ACCOUNTS	START	FINISH

MONTHLY MONEY GOALS TRACKER

MONTHLY MONEY GOALS		PROGRESS TRACKER			
1:		25%	50%	75%	100%
2:		25%	50%	75%	100%
3:		25%	50%	75%	100%
4:		25%	50%	75%	100%

WEEK	GOAL 1	GOAL 2	GOAL 3	GOAL 3
1				
2				
3				
4				

NOTES

NOTES	YES / NO
I set reasonable goals	
I met my budget goals	

MONTHLY SAVINGS PLAN

	MONTH

OPENING BALANCE	SAVINGS GOAL	SAVED

DATE	WITHDRAWAL / DEPOSIT

NOTES	REWARD

SAVINGS CHART

ITEM I AM SAVING FOR	COST	TIME FRAME

MONEY TRACKER		DATE	SAVED	BALANCE
100% ----				
75% ----				
50% ----				
25% ----				

NOTES

52 WEEK MONEY SAVING CHALLENGE

☑	WEEK	AMOUNT	BALANCE	☑	WEEK	AMOUNT	BALANCE
	1	$ 1	$ 1		27	$ 27	$ 378
	2	$ 2	$ 3		28	$ 28	$ 406
	3	$ 3	$ 6		29	$ 29	$ 435
	4	$ 4	$ 10		30	$ 30	$ 465
	5	$ 5	$ 15		31	$ 31	$ 496
	6	$ 6	$ 21		32	$ 32	$ 528
	7	$ 7	$ 28		33	$ 33	$ 561
	8	$ 8	$ 36		34	$ 34	$ 595
	9	$ 9	$ 45		35	$ 35	$ 630
	10	$ 10	$ 55		36	$ 36	$ 666
	11	$ 11	$ 66		37	$ 37	$ 703
	12	$ 12	$ 78		38	$ 38	$ 741
	13	$ 13	$ 91		39	$ 39	$ 780
	14	$ 14	$ 105		40	$ 40	$ 820
	15	$ 15	$ 120		41	$ 41	$ 861
	16	$ 16	$ 136		42	$ 42	$ 903
	17	$ 17	$ 153		43	$ 43	$ 946
	18	$ 18	$ 171		44	$ 44	$ 990
	19	$ 19	$ 190		45	$ 45	$ 1035
	20	$ 20	$ 210		46	$ 46	$ 1081
	21	$ 21	$ 231		47	$ 47	$ 1128
	22	$ 22	$ 253		48	$ 48	$ 1176
	23	$ 23	$ 276		49	$ 49	$ 1225
	24	$ 24	$ 300		50	$ 50	$ 1275
	25	$ 25	$ 325		51	$ 51	$ 1326
	26	$ 26	$ 351		52	$ 52	$ 1378

ANNUAL OVERVIEW

	INCOME	EXPENSES	SAVINGS	START BALANCE	END BALANCE
January					
February					
March					
April					
May					
June					
July					
August					
September					
October					
November					
December					
Total					

	MONTH	NOTES
Best month for income		
Lowest amount on expenses		
Highest amount of savings		
Worst month for income		
Highest amount on expenses		
Lowest amount on savings		

NOTES

2020 YEARLY PAYMENT OVERVIEW

ITEM	J	F	M	A	M	J	J	A	S	O	N	D

DEBT REPAYMENT PLAN

ACCOUNT	DUE DATE	MINIMUM DUE

CREDIT LIMIT	INTEREST RATE	CREDITOR

STARTING AMOUNT	TARGET PAYOFF DAY	ADDITIONAL INFORMATION

DATE	PAYMENT	BALANCE	NOTES

Bill Tracker

MONTH OF:

UTILITIES	BUDGET	SPENT
ELECTRIC	$	$
GAS	$	$
TRASH	$	$
INTERNET	$	$
PHONE	$	$
TOTAL	$	$

PERSONAL	BUDGET	SPENT
ENTERTAINMENT	$	$
CLOTHING	$	$
COSMETICS	$	$
LIFE INSURANCE	$	$
OTHER	$	$
TOTAL	$	$

HOME	BUDGET	SPENT
RENT/MORTGAGE	$	$
TAXES	$	$
INSURANCE	$	$
REPAIRS	$	$
TOTAL	$	$

TRANSPORTATION	BUDGET	SPENT
CAR PAYMENT	$	$
CAR INSURANCE	$	$
GAS	$	$
MAINTENANCE	$	$
TOTAL	$	$

FOOD	BUDGET	SPENT
GROCERIES	$	$
EATING OUT	$	$
TOTAL	$	$

MEDICAL	BUDGET	SPENT
DOCTOR BILLS	$	$
MEDICATION	$	$
TOTAL	$	$

GIVING	BUDGET	SPENT
TITHES	$	$
CHARITY	$	$
TOTAL	$	$

DEBTS	BUDGET	SPENT
CREDIT CARD	$	$
OTHER	$	$
TOTAL	$	$

INCOME

DATE	FROM WHERE?	AMT

CHECKING ACCOUNT

STARTING	GOAL	ENDING

SAVINGS ACCOUNT

STARTING	GOAL	ENDING

NOTES:

the monthly bill tracker

due	description	J	F	M	A	M	J	J	A	S	O	N	D

Expense Tracker

MONTH OF:

date	description	category	amount	balance
			the total	

9 781952 035791